STAGE
6
BOOK 3

THE ONE WHO WON

John Townsend

RISING ★ STARS

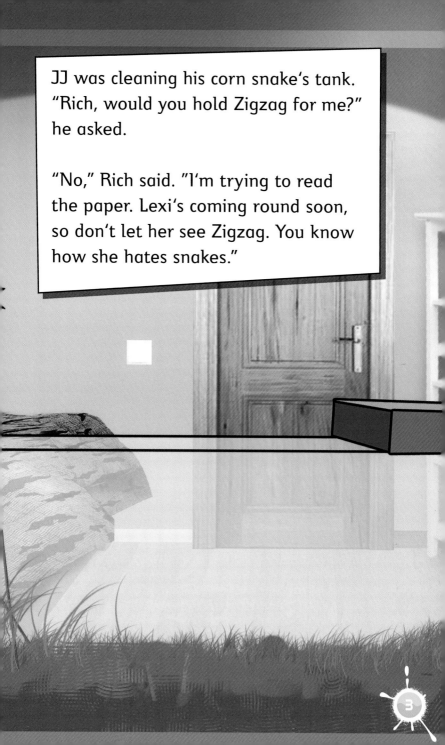

JJ was cleaning his corn snake's tank. "Rich, would you hold Zigzag for me?" he asked.

"No," Rich said. "I'm trying to read the paper. Lexi's coming round soon, so don't let her see Zigzag. You know how she hates snakes."

"If Lexi hates snakes why are you both going to the cinema tomorrow night to see *Snake Attack*? They say it's really scary and it takes a whole hour for a man to get swallowed by a python — in 3D!" JJ laughed.

Rich smiled, "Well if Lexi freaks out, I'll be there to save her — like a knight in shining armour!"

"I bet you the cost of your cinema ticket that you won't stay till the end of the film," JJ said.

"It's a deal," Rich replied, shaking JJ's hand. "I bet Lexi will be fine and that I'll be the one who wins our bet."

That night Zigzag slithered up a reed to the top of its tank. Then it slipped through a hole in the top. Soon it was sliding over JJ's bedroom carpet and out through the door.

Zigzag slid into the shoe cupboard to find a safe place. It slipped easily over the smooth wood of a floorboard.

Rich's new trainers had a secret space inside the heel. It was a place to keep money safe — but it was also safe and dark for a snake to sleep inside.

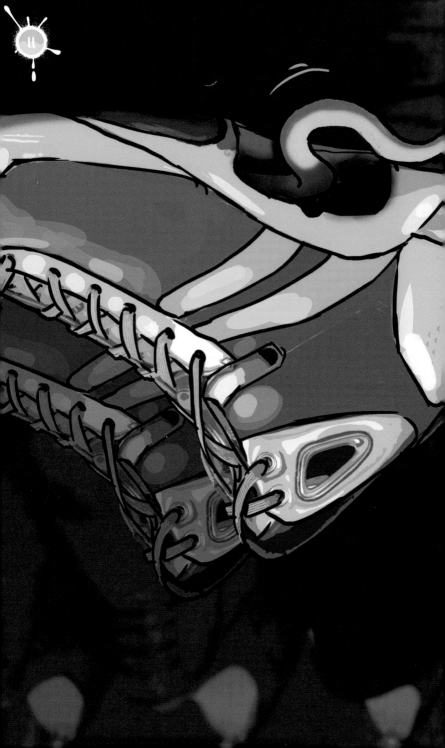

By morning Zigzag was fast asleep. No one knew about the escape in the night.

As he got dressed, JJ had other things on his mind, "Has anyone seen my red T-shirt? Have you worn it, Tasha?"

"No way!" Tasha cried. "I'd never wear your smelly T-shirt. Where did you leave it?"

"OK, don't make a scene," JJ called back. "If I knew where I had left it, I wouldn't be asking. Maybe I threw it in the wash basket."

By the evening Zigzag was still fast asleep. Rich was getting ready to go to the cinema.
As he put on his trainers he called to JJ, "Don't forget our bet. You can pay me when I get home."

In the cinema Lexi and Rich wore their 3D glasses as the film began. "I'm not sure I'm going to like this if it's got snakes in it," Lexi said.

"You'll be fine. They're not real.
At least you won't get bored!"
Rich put his arm round her.

The snakes on the screen looked scary in 3D. Lexi gripped Rich's arm tightly ... just as Zigzag began to wake up and slip out of Rich's trainer. It slithered round Lexi's ankle with a hiss ... just as Lexi looked down.

"AAAAAAH!" Lexi leapt onto her seat with a scream. "Get it off me! Shoo!"

Everyone else screamed, too! Rich grabbed hold of Zigzag.

"It's harmless!" he shouted. "It's JJ's corn snake. Where has it come from? I bet JJ did this for a joke. He'll pay for this!"

The cinema manager told Lexi and Rich to leave.

Lexi took a sip of tea, "We'll never know how that film ended." JJ laughed, "It ended with a great pay-off — cash to the one who won."

JJ was so pleased to have Zigzag home again. "I didn't play a joke on you, Rich. Honest."